Celebrate!

Easter

Mike Hirst

W

HODDER
Wayland
an imprint of Hodder
Children's Books

Celebrate!

CHINESE NEW YEAR
CHRISTMAS
DIWALI

EASTER
ID-UL-FITR
PASSOVER

This book is based on the original title **Easter**
in the **Festivals** series, published in 1997 by
Wayland Publishers Ltd.

Text copyright © 2000 Hodder Wayland
Volume copyright © 2000 Hodder Wayland

Series concept: Polly Goodman

Published in Great Britain in 2000 by Hodder
Wayland, an imprint of Hodder Children's Books.

This paperback edition published in 2002
Reprinted in 2002

A catalogue record for this book is available from
the British Library.

ISBN 0 7502 4044 X

Printed and bound in Hong Kong

Hodder Children's Books
A division of Hodder Headline Limited
338 Euston Road, London NW1 3BH

Picture acknowledgements
AKG 6, 7 top, 8, 16 top; The Bridgeman Art
Library 7 bottom; Britstock 10, 13, 22, 27 bottom; Chapel Studios (Zul Mukhida) 20; Chris
Fairclough 17; J Allan Cash 15; Sonia Halliday
24; Robert Harding 5 right; Impact cover top
right; Magnum 5 left, 23; St Albans and
Harpenden Observer 4 top; Tony Stone cover
middle, 12, 16 bottom (James Davis), 18 bottom, 26, 28; Trip 4 middle, bottom left and
right, 11, 14, 18 top, 21 top, 25, 27 top, 29; Zefa
cover top left, bottom middle and left, title
page, 19, 21. Border artwork is by Tim Mayer.

Contents

Words that appear in **bold** are explained in the glossary on page 30.

Easter around the World

◄ These Christians, in Britain, have come from many different churches to join together for an Easter Monday service.

▲ In Romania, these Christians are waiting for Easter Sunday to begin.

◄ Children with palm leaf crosses in Benin, West Africa.

◄ In Jerusalem, Christians carry a wooden cross through the streets on Good Friday.

There are Christians in almost every part of the world. They all celebrate Easter, but in many different ways. In many countries, Easter Monday is a national holiday.

▲ An Easter Sunday service in the American city of Washington DC.

▲ Palm Sunday in Peru. The men are holding a statue of Jesus on a donkey, to remind them of the Palm Sunday story (see page 14).

The Easter Story

Christians are followers of Jesus Christ. This important religious leader lived 2,000 years ago, in a country called **Palestine**. At that time, Palestine was part of the Roman Empire.

Christians believe that Jesus was the son of God. He was a famous teacher and even today, Christians try to behave in the ways that Jesus showed them.

Easter is the time when Christians remember the last week of Jesus' life.

▲ The Easter story began when Jesus rode into the city of Jerusalem on a donkey. Many people were happy to see him.

The Easter story is a sad story because Jesus was killed. But the story has a very happy ending, because Jesus came back to life and visited his friends and followers once more. He did not die at all, but went back up to Heaven to be with God, his father.

Some people in Palestine did not like the things that Jesus taught. They told the Romans that Jesus was a wicked man. Even one of Jesus' friends turned against him. His name was Judas.

The ruler of Palestine was called Pontius Pilate. He ordered his soldiers to kill Jesus.

▲ This stone carving shows Pontius Pilate, the Roman ruler, sitting on the left.

Gospels

The Easter story is written in four books of the **Bible**. These books are called the **Gospels**.

◀ Saint Mark wrote one of the four Gospels.

On the day Jesus was to be killed, the Roman soldiers nailed him to a big wooden cross and left him to die. This way of killing someone is called **crucifixion.**

When Jesus had died, his friends took his body away. They wrapped it in cloth and put it inside a **tomb**. The tomb was a cave, with a big stone in front.

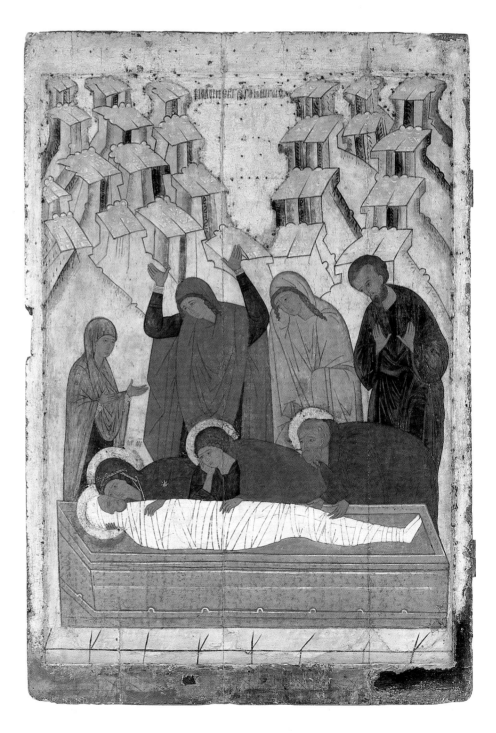

► This painting shows Jesus' body wrapped in cloth. His mother and friends are weeping.

Jesus rises from the dead

Two days later, some friends of Jesus went to visit his tomb. The stone was rolled away from the entrance, but Jesus was not there. He had come back to life again! This is now called the **Resurrection**.

▲ Some Christians believe this church, in the town of Jerusalem, Israel, is built in the exact place where Jesus was buried.

Jesus Returns to his Followers

Jesus visited many of his friends and followers when he came back to life. Then he left the Earth again and went up to **Heaven**. But he told his followers that his **spirit** would always stay with them.

Getting Ready for Easter

The Easter festival takes place in March or April every year. It is on a different date from year to year.

Lent

Just before Easter, there is a time called Lent. Lent lasts for forty days.

▲ New-born lambs are a sign of new life at Easter time.

During Lent, people remember the time when Jesus spent forty days and forty nights living alone in the desert. During this time, he **fasted**, which means he did not eat any food.

Some Christians make their own fast at Lent. They usually give up one thing they like, such as sweets or chocolate.

For many Christians, Lent is a quiet time. It is a good time to pray and think about how to lead a good life.

▼ These people, in Romania, are waiting for dawn on Easter Sunday, after a special church service.

Ash Wednesday

Ash Wednesday is the first day of Lent. Ash reminds people that their bodies turn to dust in the end. It helps them be sorry for their sins.

Shrove Tuesday

The last day before Lent is called Shrove Tuesday. In the past, Christians had a big party on Shrove Tuesday. They ate up any food that they would not eat during the fast for Lent. Many customs still continue today.

◄ In Italy, the people of Venice have a carnival before Lent. They dress up in special clothes and wear masks.

Mardi Gras

In France, Shrove Tuesday is called Mardi Gras, which means 'Fat Tuesday'. Today there are Mardi Gras celebrations in the city of New Orleans, USA and in Sydney, Australia.

▲ Many places in South America have a carnival before Lent. The most famous is in Rio de Janeiro, Brazil.

Pancakes

Long ago, people in Britain started making pancakes on Shrove Tuesday. They wanted to use up all their cooking fat before Lent.

Today, British people still make pancakes on 'Pancake Day'. Some villages even have a race. Competitors hold a frying pan as they run, and toss a pancake up in the air as they go.

Holy Week Begins

The last week of Lent is called Holy Week. The first day of Holy Week is called Palm Sunday.

Christians remember how Jesus entered the city of Jerusalem. The people were so happy to see him that they waved branches of palm trees as he rode by on a donkey.

Today, in many churches, people make crosses made out of palm leaves.

► These children are taking palm crosses to a church in Benin, West Africa.

14

Maundy Thursday

As Holy Week goes on, it becomes more serious.

On Maundy Thursday, Christians remember Jesus' last meal with his friends, called 'The Last Supper'. They also think about Judas, who betrayed Jesus by giving him away to his enemies.

▲ In Britain, the Queen goes to a special church service on Maundy Thursday. She gives gifts of money, called 'Maundy money'.

The Flight of the Bells

In France, church bells do not ring on the two days between Maundy Thursday and Easter Sunday. Parents tell their children that the bells have flown off to Rome to see the **Pope**.

Good Friday

On Good Friday, Christians remember the day that Jesus was killed.

Jesus was killed by soldiers who nailed him to a wooden cross. Today, the cross is an important sign for Christians.

You can see crosses in churches and religious buildings. Many Christians wear a cross on a chain. At Easter, people even eat hot cross buns – a pastry with a cross shape on top.

▲ Many artists have painted the Crucifixion of Jesus.

► In Greece, Christians put a tomb in the middle of their church on Good Friday.

The Crucifixion

In some countries, such as Spain, people act out the story of the Crucifixion. They stop fourteen times along the way to pray and think about how Jesus suffered.

An Easter Garden

Jesus' body was put in a tomb in a garden. In many parts of Europe, children make a model of the garden, called an Easter Garden.

▲ In this Easter garden, Jesus has come back to life. He is speaking to a follower.

Happy Easter

On Easter Sunday, Christians celebrate the day that Jesus came back to life. This event has a special name. It is called the Resurrection.

Many people stay up the night before Easter Sunday to welcome the start of the day.

▲ At midnight just before Easter Sunday, the priest passes around an Easter candle. Soon everyone will have a candle to light up the church.

◄ Many people go to Saint Peter's Square in Rome on Easter Sunday. They go to see the Pope, who is the leader of the Roman Catholic church.

Easter Sunday is one of the happiest days of the year. Christians meet in church to celebrate.

Easter Sunday is also the end of Lent. In Ireland, people used to cook a chicken on Saturday night. The food was ready to eat the minute that Lent was over.

▼ This boy is part of an Easter Sunday service in Jerusalem.

The Easter Flower

The white lily is a special Easter flower. White is a sign of purity and goodness.

Egg Sunday

On Easter Sunday, many people give presents of Easter eggs to their family and friends.

In some countries, parents hide Easter eggs around their home and hold Easter-egg hunts. Children race to find the eggs. Parents tell their children that the Easter Hare has hidden the eggs.

► These girls have found Easter eggs in their garden.

The first Easter eggs were hard-boiled eggs. In some countries, people still make these hard-boiled eggs.

Hard-boiled eggs are dipped in food dye to give them a bright colour. Some people also paint patterns on their eggs.

Nowadays, chocolate eggs are a popular Easter present.

▲ These eggs have been dyed red for Easter.

Eggs

Easter eggs are a sign of new life. They remind Christians of the Resurrection.

A basket of brightly coloured eggs. ▲

Easter Monday

People celebrate Easter Monday with many different customs around the world.

▼ The President of the USA has an egg-rolling competition for children. It takes place in the gardens of the White House, in Washington DC.

Egg Rolling

Egg rolling happens in Scotland, Switzerland and many other places too.

The egg rollers stand at the top of a slope. They let their eggs go, so that they roll away. The first egg to reach the bottom is the winner.

Ducking Monday

In Hungary, Easter Monday is called Ducking Monday. Young men used to dip their girlfriends in a pond for a joke.

Gold Eggs

A Russian jeweller called Peter Fabergé lived over 100 years ago. He made beautiful gold eggs, decorated with jewels. Only very rich people could afford these Easter eggs.

▲ This beautiful Easter egg is decorated with gold and jewels. Can you see the year when it was made?

Another old custom in Britain was 'heaving'. People ran after strangers and lifted them up. The strangers had to give money to charity before they were put down again.

Pictures and Plays

In the past, many people never went to school. They did not have books and could not read the Easter story for themselves.

Passion plays

People put on plays to tell the Easter story, so that everyone could learn about the meaning of Easter. These plays were called **passion plays**.

▶ This stained-glass window tells the Easter story in pictures.
Can you see Jesus on the cross in the top pictures?

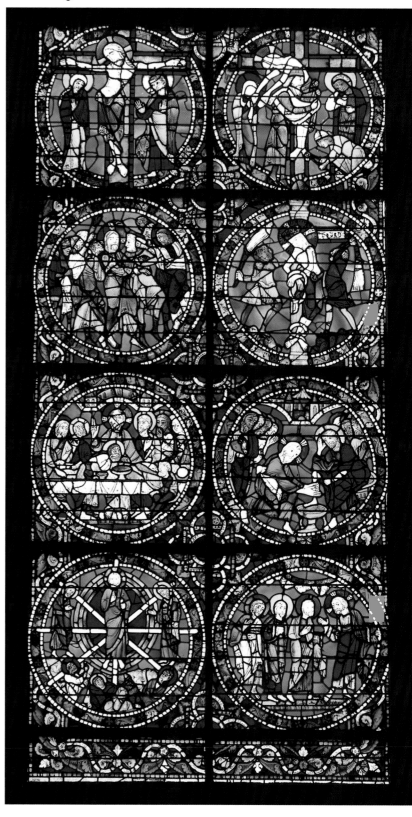

Some places still have passion plays, even today. In Britain, you can see them at York. In the USA, there are passion plays at Strasburg in Virginia and Eureka Springs in Arizona.

Plague Promise

One of the most famous passion plays takes place in the German village of Oberammergau. Over 350 years ago, many villagers caught a terrible illness called the plague. They promised that when the illness went away, they would perform a passion play every ten years. This was their way of saying thank you to God.

▲ This boy is a soldier in a passion play in Spain.

Easter Food

Many Christians eat special foods at Easter.
Italians eat salty biscuits called pretzels.
Russians have little pancakes called blini.
In Denmark, people eat Shrovetide buns.

In Britain, people eat hot cross buns. The cross on the top reminds them of how Jesus died on a cross.

Many years ago in Britain, churches gave hot cross buns to poor people on Good Friday.

◄ Hot cross buns with melted butter.

◄ A simnel cake. Can you count the rounds of almond paste?

Simnel cake

Simnel cake is a special fruit cake. It has eleven round shapes of almond paste on top. Each round stands for one of the followers of Jesus in the Easter story.

Passion Fruit

The passion fruit was named after the shape of its flower. Part of the flower looks like the nails that held Jesus to the cross. Another part looks like the crown of thorns that Jesus wore on his head.

▲ A flower of the passion fruit plant.

The Christian Calendar

November to December
ADVENT
Advent lasts for just over three weeks in December. It is the time to get ready for Christmas.

25 December
CHRISTMAS DAY
The day when Jesus Christ was born. For most people this is 25 December, but some Christians celebrate on 6 January.

6 January
EPIPHANY
This day is twelve days after Christmas Day. It is when the wise men brought presents to the baby Jesus.

February
SHROVE TUESDAY
The last day before the start of Lent. People celebrate by eating pancakes or joining carnivals.

February to March/April
LENT
Lent lasts for 40 days before Easter.

February
ASH WEDNESDAY
The first day of Lent.

March/April
HOLY WEEK
The last week of Lent.

March/April
PALM SUNDAY
The first day of Holy Week.

March/April
MAUNDY THURSDAY
Thursday in Holy Week.

March/April
GOOD FRIDAY
The day when people remember Jesus' crucifixion.

March/April
EASTER
On Easter Sunday, Christians remember the Resurrection, when Jesus came back to life.

May
ASCENSION DAY
Christians celebrate Jesus going back up to Heaven, forty days after Easter.

June
PENTECOST
After Jesus went up to Heaven, God sent the **Holy Spirit** to help his followers on Earth. The Holy Spirit came down to Earth at Pentecost.

Harvest Festival
In September or October, churches are filled with flowers and fruit. Christians thank God for giving them food.

Glossary

Bible   The Christian holy book. The Bible tells Christians how God wants them to live.

Crucifixion   The name for the way Jesus was killed on a cross.

fasted   Gave up some or all food.

Gospels   The parts of the Bible that tell us about the life of Jesus.

Heaven   The place where God lives with his son Jesus. Christians believe that they will go to be with Jesus in heaven when they die.

Holy Spirit   The part of God which came to be on Earth after Jesus went back to Heaven. Christians believe that the Holy Spirit helps them to lead good lives.

Palestine   The name of the country where Jesus lived.

Passion play   A play that tells the Easter story.

pilgrimage   A special journey.

Pope   The leader of the Roman Catholic Church.

Resurrection   The name for how Jesus came back to life after he was killed.

Roman Empire   A vast area around the Mediterranean Sea ruled by the Romans from 27 BC until AD 476.

sins   Things that people have done wrong.

spirit   The soul, which is separate from the body.

tomb   A place where a dead body is kept.

Finding Out More

BOOKS TO READ

A Feast of Festivals by Hugo Slim
(Marshall Pickering, 1996)
A Flavour of France by Teresa Fisher
(Wayland, 1998)
Celebration! by Barnabas and Anabel
Kindersley (Dorling Kindersley, 1997)
Celebrate Christian Festivals by Jan
Thompson (Heinemann, 1995)
Christianity by John Logan (Wayland,
1995)
Christian Festival Cookbooks (Hodder
Wayland, 2000)
Christian Festival Tales by Saviour
Pirotta (Hodder Wayland, 2000)
Feasts and Festivals by Jacqueline
Dineen (Dragons World, 1995)
What do we know about Christianity
(Macdonald Young Books, 1996)
The World of Festivals by Philip Steele
(Macdonald Young Books, 1996)

OTHER RESOURCE MATERIAL
Festivals Worksheets by Albany Bilbe
and Liz George (Wayland, 1998)
25 photocopiable, copyright-free
worksheets on the topic of festivals.
The Festival Year: an annual calendar
of multifaith festivals (Festival Shop).

USEFUL ADDRESSES

Catholic Information Service,
74 Gallow Hill Lane,
Abbotts Langley, Herts, WD5 OBZ

Christian Education Movement,
Royal Buildings, Victoria Street,
Derby DE1 1GW
Tel: 01332 296655

Church of England Information Office,
Church House, Deans Yard,
London N10, 1PR

Committee for Extra-Diocesan
Affairs, Russian Orthodox Cathedral,
Ennismore Gardens, London SW7

The Festival Shop, 56 Poplar Road,
Kings Heath, Birmingham B14 7AG
Tel: 0121 444 0444

SHAP Working Party on World
Religions and The National Society's
RE Centre, 36 Causton Street,
London SW1P 4AU
Tel: 0207 932 1194

Index